A CALGARY ALBUM

Mark & Janice Kozub

A CALGARY
Album

Glimpses of the
Way We Were

A HOUNSLOW BOOK
A MEMBER OF THE DUNDURN GROUP
TORONTO · OXFORD

Publisher: Anthony Hawke
Editor: Julian Walker
Design: Jennifer Scott
Printer: Transcontinental

Canadian Cataloguing in Publication Data

Kozub, Mark
    A Calgary album: glimpses of the way we were

ISBN 0-88882-224-3

1. Calgary (Alta.) — History — Pictorial works. I. Kozub, Janice. II. Title.

FC3697.37.K69 2001   971.23'38'00222   C00-931878-X   F1079.5C35K69 2001

1   2   3   4   5   05   04   03   02   01

THE CANADA COUNCIL | LE CONSEIL DES ARTS
FOR THE ARTS | DU CANADA
SINCE 1957 | DEPUIS 1957

Canada

ONTARIO ARTS COUNCIL
CONSEIL DES ARTS DE L'ONTARIO

We acknowledge the support of the **Canada Council for the Arts** and the **Ontario Arts Council** for our publishing program. We also acknowledge the financial support of the **Government of Canada** through the **Book Publishing Industry Development Program**, **The Association for the Export of Canadian Books**, and the **Government of Ontario** through the **Ontario Book Publishers Tax Credit** program.

Printed and bound in Canada.⊛
Printed on recycled paper.

www.dundurn.com

Front Cover Photo: Glenbow Archives, Calgary, Canada NA-3354-9 Photographer: Davis, J., Calgary, Alberta
Back Cover Photo (left): Glenbow Archives, Calgary, Canada NB-50-62 Photographer: Sambrook, I.W., Calgary, Alberta
Back Cover Photo (right): Glenbow Archives, Calgary, Canada NB-16-417 Photographer: Oliver, W.J., Calgary, Alberta

Dundurn Press
8 Market Street
Suite 200
Toronto, Ontario, Canada
M5E 1M6

Dundurn Press
73 Lime Walk
Headington, Oxford,
England
OX3 7AD

Dundurn Press
2250 Military Road
Tonawanda NY
U.S.A. 14150

To our parents, grandparents, and all other hard workers and daydreamers alike

who breathed new and vibrant life into the prairies

Acknowledgements

FIRST OF ALL, A BIG THANKS must go to Jo-Anne Christensen and Dennis Shappka, authors of *An Edmonton Album: Glimpses of the Way We Were,* for laying the groundwork. (We still owe you dinner!) Our appreciation also goes to Tony Hawke, a publisher with vision and insight.

As well, the mammoth job of searching for just the right photographs was made infinitely easier by people like Lisa Atkinson, Archival Program Manager at the University of Calgary Archives and Pat Molesky at the Glenbow Museum. The staff of the latter must have spent countless hours putting together what is a thoroughly comprehensive web-based archive.

Finally, we would like to thank hospitable Calgarians like Sandra Runge and Robert and Suzanne Toth. (Thanks for the fine photograph, Rob!)

The Spirit of the Pioneer Lives On

THERE IS SOMETHING WE LEARNED WHILE researching and writing this book. With our cushy Friday nights of Chinese take-out and videos, our generation has lost the rough grit that characterised the settlers of Alberta. Sad, but true. While the twenty-first century arrives fraught with its own unique forms of stress (pollution, downsizing, ever-changing technology), life in the 1880s was particularly difficult — especially here in Alberta.

Back then, this undefined part of Western Canada was considered to be best left alone unless you were a hardened trapper. Those with vision, however, braved the elements and became pioneers of a way of life known as much for its hardships as its sense of promise.

Calgary, to this day, stands as a monument to the struggles of the pioneer. If John Glenn, the first rancher to settle at First Creek in 1873, could have crafted himself a time machine — this resourceful man did, after all, build the first stone fireplaces for the old Bow River fort — would he have believed his eyes? Just how baffled would this pioneer be by this hustling, bustling city full of cars, cell phones, Web surfers and software developers? And what exactly would he make of the nostalgic cowboy hats donned during the famed Calgary Stampede?

It's quite possible that the pioneers who built this city would prefer the slower life, the good old days when relaxing meant taking a leisurely walk in the field.

Few can argue the fact that the lives of twenty-first century adults are, to say the least, more comfortable than those of John Glenn's time. We may never comprehend how hard our parents worked or how back-breaking the chores of our grandparents were. All we know for certain, as we look at the new and ever-changing landscape of this sprawling city, is that we are still filled with a sense of promise. The pioneers of yesterday are gone, but their spirit lives on, a spirit captured on film in these glimpses of the way we were.

**A trip back to 1891,
a time when Calgary was hardly
the urban metropolis it is today.**

B3191,
Provincial Archives of Alberta
Photographer: Brown, Earnest

Frontier Beginnings

U NTIL NEARLY THE END OF THE nineteenth century, the popular line of thought amongst politicians and the general public was that Western Canada (or Rupert's Land, as it was known) only held allure for those who preferred life under extreme conditions. Or as Sir George Simpson, governor of the Hudson's Bay Company, told a British Royal Commission in 1857: the West should be left to the trapper and trader. Forever.

Fort Calgary, 1876

Glenbow Archives, Calgary, Canada   ND-8-252
Photographer: Oliver, W.J., Calgary, Alberta

F-Troop, North West Mounted Police at

Fort Calgary, 1876

Glenbow Archives, Calgary, Canada NA-354-10

Photographer unknown

Captain E.A. Brisebois of the North West Mounted Police, photographed here in 1876, tried in vain to ensure that the Bow River fort was named after him. Instead, it was named Fort Calgary. The name Calgary is thought to have been derived from a Gaelic word meaning "Bay Farm."

Glenbow Archives, Calgary, Canada NA-828-1
Photographer unknown

Calgary's Citizen of the Century

IN 1975, DECADES AFTER HIS DEATH, James Walker was awarded the rather prestigious title of Calgary's Citizen of the Year. It was Walker who established the Bow River Saw Mills Company in 1881. As business grew, the company would go on to become a key employer in the region. By 1883, Walker was placing advertisements for as many as twenty carpenters at a time. Their pay was $3.50 a day.

In years to come, taking a cue from the success of Walker's company, competition came in the form of the Eau Claire Lumber Company run by Peter Prince.

In 1894, the two companies had together sold over one million feet of timber.

Colonel James Walker's saw mill, photographed sometime between 1880 and 1883.

Walker is the man on the far right.

Glenbow Archives, Calgary, Canada NA-1478-1

Photographer unknown

Shopping on the Frontier

IN THE LATE 1800S, NOT SO long after Sir George Simpson's remark about Western Canada being best left to the trapper, the I. G. Baker store was one of the first major buildings erected — a sure sign that settlers were ready to move in. The first Hudson's Bay Company trading store was carried by river to Calgary from its original location in the mountains.

The I.G. Baker store, built in October 1875 and moved to 9th Avenue and 1st Street Southeast in 1883 and 1884.

Notable personalities in the photo include (from left): Angus Sparrow, John L. Bowen, I.G. Baker (manager), "Ghost River" McDonald (father of D.P.), Mr. Playfair, A.P. Patrick, Second Deputy Sheriff Fitzgerald, and Willie Bowmen (sixth from the right).

Glenbow Archives, Calgary, Canada NA-345-18
Photographer unknown

THE ORIGINAL HUDSON'S BAY C?'S STORE IN CALGARY
1884-1891

In 1875, The Hudson's Bay Company's trading post was located at the Bow River Fort. In 1884, its first store opened near the Royal Canadian Mounted Police fort in east Calgary.

ROYAL MAIL LINE

LEESON & SCOTT, Proprietors.

QU'APPELLE & CALGARY, N.W.T.

Stages leave Qu'Appelle Station every Wednesday morning for Prince Albert, Battleford and Fort Pitt.

They leave Calgary every alternate Friday morning, from the 20th March, for Edmonton and Fort Saskatchewan.

Returning from Fort Pitt route every Wednesday morning, and from Edmonton every alternate Friday morning.

For particulars apply to

LEESON & SCOTT, Qu'Appelle and Calgary.

An advertisement for the Royal Mail Line, Qu'Appelle & Calgary, 1885, from Burns and Elliott's directory.

A Different Kind of Shopping Experience ...

IN CALGARY AND ITS SURROUNDING RURAL areas, as in other parts of the world, the way we shop for goods is being reinvented by the advent of "super malls" and, more recently, e-commerce. Before the age of technology, shopping was about more than just browsing the store shelves or the newest web-site. It was a chance to chat with the store clerk and other shoppers or to catch up on local news and, more often, local gossip.

The goods one could find in Calgary's first Hudson's Bay Company store were far from metropolitan. Instead, the shelves were most often stacked with flintlock muskets, carrot tobacco in three-pound rolls, and items specific to the Company such as hooded duffle capotes.

Interestingly, at the start of the 1900s, a hungry consumer could also buy something called Orange Meat. Today, this same product is still on grocery store shelves, believe it or not ... only now we refer to it simply as Corn Flakes.

A twenty minute time exposure shot taken of the interior of the
Hudson's Bay Company store in the spring of 1904.

Glenbow Archives, Calgary, Canada NA-121-1
Photographer: Snider, K.W., Calgary, Alberta

"Cow-town," Indeed!

W HILE AGRICULTURE STILL HOLDS A PROMINENT place in modern Calgary's industry, the golden age of the open range is long gone. In 1896, the Walrond Ranch Company saw profits exceeding $133,000 — enough money in those days to make a modern-day oil tycoon turn green with envy. By 1906, as many as three million acres of Alberta land were ploughed by nearly a thousand different individuals or companies, and there were approximately a million head of cattle.

A cattle round up in the Calgary area, 1890.

Glenbow Archives, Calgary, Canada NA-1905-18
Photograph: Mather, T.H.

A Bad Time to be a Rancher ...

WHILE THE LATE NINETEENTH CENTURY MAY now be considered the most prosperous time to have been on the range, in 1887 the entire cattle industry was hit hard by the most disastrous winter ever experienced in North America. By spring, few ranchers found their farms untouched. In fact, most had lost at least 40 percent of their once prosperous herds — some lost as much as 75 percent!

To make matters worse, some herds across the prairies were suffering from the effects of the skin disease mange. By the time the winter chill peaked, many animals were almost entirely without hair.

Even in the year 1889, Stephen Avenue was an odd place to find a cow.

Glenbow Archives, Calgary, Canada NA-2864-13233

Photographer unknown

FIRE!

On November 5th, 1886 at 5 a.m., at the northwest corner of 9th Avenue (then Atlantic Avenue) and Centre Street (then McTavish Street), behind Parrish & Son's flour and feed store, a few innocent sparks signalled the start of a fire that would rage its way over 1st Street West, east over 9th Avenue and southwest to 8th Avenue (then Stephen Avenue). Weather conditions were against the citizens of Calgary and a number of prominent buildings were burnt to a cinder. Among the eighteen businesses wiped from the face of Calgary were the Pullman Saloon, Union Hotel, and Dunne & Lineham's old butcher shop. The Royal Hotel may have been burnt to the ground, too, had it not been for volunteers who frantically protected it with wet blankets.

Total damages cost a then staggering $103,200. Less than a quarter of that was covered by insurance policies. The cause of the fire is, to this day, unknown.

The Empire Hotel on fire at night.

Glenbow Archives, Calgary, Canada NB-16-427

Photographer: Oliver, W.J., Calgary, Alberta

The Empire Hotel.

Glenbow Archives, Calgary, Canada NB-16-426

Photographer: Oliver, W.J., Calgary, Alberta

Even a respected fire chief likes to clown around! Here, Calgary's fire chief from the years 1898 — 1933, James "Cappy" Smart, hammed it up for the cameras, dressed as a Scottish comedian known as Sir Harry Lauder.

Glenbow Archives, Calgary, Canada NA-2316-3
Photographer unknown

**The Calgary Fire Department's vehicles photographed outside of the
old Fire Station No.1.**

Glenbow Archives, Calgary, Canada NA-2854-116

Photographer unknown

The Sandstone Era

AFTER THE FIRE OF 1886, CAUTIOUS Calgarians began to use a new type of construction: buildings were now being crafted from sandstone. One of the first to be built was the courthouse, followed by the erection of a proper fire house, located on the north side of 7th Avenue between Centre Street and 1st Street East. Many homes were also built using sandstone. Sir James A. Lougheed, a popular businessman of the time, built his sturdy family home, named Beaulieu, using the trendy material in 1889.

The Sandstone Era was, however, a short-lived one. By 1914, the construction industry was choosing alternative forms of building materials, including brick and limestone. One of the last buildings in Calgary to be built in this style was The Mewata Armouries in 1917.

Beaulieu — the Lougheed family residence in the early 1900s.

Glenbow Archives, Calgary, Canada NA-789-157

Photographer unknown

Riding the Rails

O N JULY 21, 1890, THE HONOURABLE Edgar Dewdney, Minister of the Interior, was spotted by many in a curious pose for a man of such stature: he was witnessed digging up the Albertan soil with a shovel. The occasion was one of considerable impact: Dewdney had the honour of turning the first sod for the Calgary-Edmonton railway (construction of which would be completed the following year).

At the turn of the century, Calgarians hoped the railway would lay the tracks towards a life of greater prosperity and growth. A short railway boom occurred from 1910 to 1914 with the construction of the two transcontinental lines, the Grand Trunk Pacific and the Canadian Northern. The price of land near the terminals and proposed rights-of-way escalated greatly — often the price was over $1,000 per frontage foot.

The Calgary Herald has once stated that it was "the duty of every man, woman and child to further the cause of railway development in Alberta." Unfortunately, the railway boom wasn't as prosperous as everyone had hoped. Both the Grand Trunk Pacific and the Canadian Northern felt the blow of a depression following 1913.

The Honourable Edgar Dewdney, Minister of the Interior, turning the first sod.

Glenbow Archives, Calgary, Canada NA-237-8

Photographer: Smyth, S.A., Calgary, Alberta

Led by Number 87, four locomotives arrive in Calgary, 1883.

(From left): W. McLeod (third), J.G. Fidler (fourth), Arthur Denman (seventh), Len Cockle (twelfth), James Geddles (thirteenth), Peter Menzies (fourteenth), J. Bellamy (fifteenth), Thomas Craig (seventeenth), and Hugh B. Gilmour (eighteenth).

Glenbow Archives, Calgary, Canada NA-967-11

Photographer unknown

Calgary Incorporated

CALGARY WAS INCORPORATED AS A TOWN in 1884. A decade later, the city exceeded the necessary amount of 2,500 citizens and it received official city status.

A view of Calgary from the Elbow River in 1884.

Glenbow Archives, Calgary, Canada NA-1038-1

Photographer: Gardner and Company, Brooklyn, New York

A view of Calgary in 1912. The old General Hospital, built in 1894 and located at 12th Avenue and

6th Street South East, is in the foreground.

Glenbow Archives, Calgary, Canada NA-2288-1

Photographer unknown

Lifestyles of the Rich and Famous

CALGARY'S ELITE ENJOYED ALL THE THRILLS the late nineteenth century had to offer. The city's wealthier and more affluent citizens enjoyed forming exclusive private societies that often did little more than mimic their counterparts in more fashionable cities. The Calgary Turf Club and the Calgary Operatic Society (which brought to the stage the city's first operetta, *The Pirates of Penzance*) attempted to bring a sense of refinement and culture to the young city.

Hull's Opera House, circa 1893 – 1897.

Glenbow Archives, Calgary, Canada NA-468-4
Photographer: Wing, W.E., Calgary, Alberta

The cast of *The Pirates of Penzance*, February of 1896.
(Clockwise, beginning at top): Mrs. Gosnell, Miss E. Janes, G. Tempest,
J.L. Johnson, J.J. Young, S. Saunders, Miss J. M. Sherriff, J. Dennis, G.A.
Macdonald, C. Smith. (Centre): Miss L. Rankin.

Glenbow Archives, Calgary, Canada NA-1426-1
Photographer unknown

Raise Your Spirits

DISRUPTIVE AND DISORDERLY BEHAVIOUR BY DRUNKEN railway construction workers in the Prairie West added fuel to the fire of the Temperance Movement at the turn of the century. Concern about crime, unemployment, violence, and, of course, religious principles helped organisations such as the American Woman's Christian Temperance Union to gain membership across the dominion. The influence of such groups on politicians would eventually result in the prohibition of the sale of alcohol for a brief period during and after the First World War.

Where could thirsty patrons go to escape the pressures put upon them by prohibitionists? The Palace Hotel Bar, of course!

A view of Centre Street around 1903. To the left is the Palace Hotel.

Glenbow Archives, Calgary, Canada NA-2031-2

Photographer unknown

The bar at the King George Hotel, located at 124-9th Avenue South West, circa 1910.

Working Women

I N 1917, WOMEN DIDN'T HAVE A lot of career options. You could choose to be a nurse, a school teacher, a housewife … or, perhaps, a prostitute. Those who claimed that Calgary was free of those who practised the world's oldest profession or other less noble occupations were either mistaken, mislead, or were lying. Their opinions were, however, shared by Police Chief Tom English who declared that there were NO illegal saloons, NO gambling houses (virtually) and most certainly NO brothels! Indeed, right within the city limits there were a fair number of well-known houses of ill repute. English was dismissed in 1909 during a reorganisation of the police force. Public drunkenness and prostitution had proliferated during the time of his tenure.

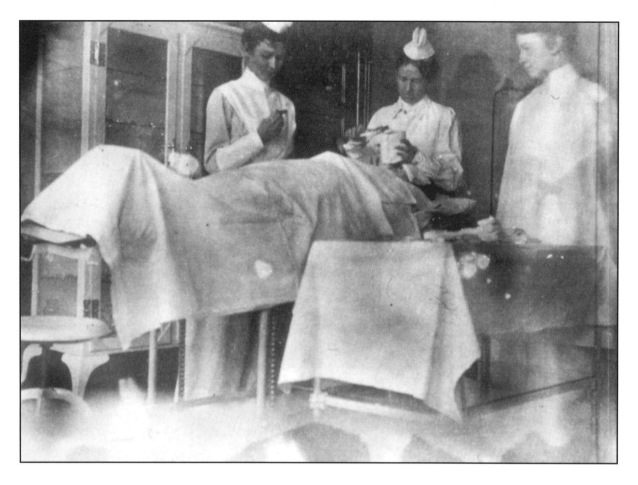

Nurses in an operating room, in 1903, administering anaesthetic.

Glenbow Archives, Calgary, Canada NA-2600-49

Photographer unknown

(From left): Air pilot Katherine Stinson, Police Chief Alfred Cuddy, G.C. King, and Nat Christie, general manager of the Calgary Exhibition and Stampede.

Glenbow Archives, Calgary, Canada NA-2354-7

Photographer: Ring, W.W., Calgary, Alberta

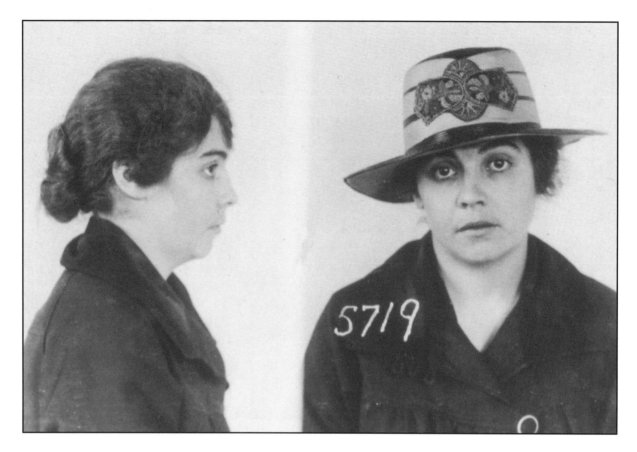

A police identification photo of Jenny Lebousky on June 21, 1917. Jenny went by such aliases as Jennie Johnson or "Babe" Johnson. This twenty-three year old prostitute had quite a criminal past. Her charges included being an inmate of a disorderly house (1912), being disorderly on street (1912), robbery (1916), and a multitude of other vagrancy charges.

Glenbow Archives, Calgary, Canada NA-625-11

Photographer: Calgary City Police

Police Chief Tom English (fourth from left) and officers, circa 1900.

Glenbow Archives, Calgary, Canada   NA-1447-24

(Photograph copied from PB-628-1)

A Capital Idea?

W HY WASN'T CALGARY, THE PROVINCE'S FIRST city, chosen to be the capital of Alberta? This is a question that has been asked ever since Edmonton was given that distinction. The story is one of politics and power and shows how a cunning politician can influence the polls in his favour. More simply, the tale of why Calgary was not chosen to be the capital is about a man who loved his hometown.

It was the duty of the Minister of the Interior in Ottawa to fix provincial constituencies. When Alberta became a province under Sir Wilfrid Laurier's government, the minister fulfilling this duty was Frank Olivier (who brought Edmonton its first printing press and founded the Edmonton *Bulletin* in 1880). Olivier's political influence gave Edmonton the advantage as electoral boundaries were being set. After the new maps were drawn, the northern half of Alberta had a larger population. In 1905, Olivier's cherished hometown became the provincial capital.

School Spirit

THE CALGARY-EDMONTON RIVALRY TOOK ON many forms over the years. For instance, Edmonton was given the honour of being the site for the University of Alberta in 1906. The Normal School opened its doors to students in Calgary that same year. This was a facility where students could receive the necessary training to become teachers, instead of going to university. Two years later, it moved to a new building and re-named itself the Calgary Normal School (for fear that it might otherwise be confused with the Normal School in Edmonton). It was relocated to the centre of the city in 1922, residing on the third floor of the west wing of the Provincial Institute of Technology and Arts (now SAIT, Southern Alberta Institute of Technology).

It was during this early period of academic growth that the City of Calgary showed enough faith to invest the sum of $150,000 for the creation of its own university. However, students and teachers alike would have to wait until after the end of the Second World War before the first step towards this goal took place. In 1945, teacher-training schools across Alberta were put under one umbrella and the school became part of the Faculty of Education of the University of Alberta.

After twenty years of waiting through gradual expansion (adding new programs and moving to its present campus), what had recently become the Calgary Branch of the University of Alberta finally became an autonomous institution on April 15th, 1966. Thanks to the ceaseless work of various lobby groups (and the occasional student hi-jinx), the city could finally boast about the University of Calgary.

A proposed layout for a Calgary university, planned by acclaimed landscape architect Mr. Dunington-Grubb, circa 1912.

85.025, University of Calgary Archives

The Normal School choir, 1942.

91.023, University of Calgary Archives

ᴬCALGARY*Album*

ENGINEERING &

ARTS & SCIENCE BUILDING

Sometimes, there is no education like that learned from the real world. Consider this quick lesson in politics …

Ever since the provincial university was established, there have been some who firmly believe one man was responsible for the fact that Calgary was overlooked: the Honourable Alexander C. Rutherford, Alberta's first premier and minister of education.

It was Rutherford who initiated the act to create a university (during the first session of 1905). The government decided that the new institution would be placed upon 258 acres on the south side of the Saskatchewan River in Strathcona: which happened to be the premier's constituency!

Did these two Engineering, Arts and Science students in 1958 feel the province was making a donkey out of Calgary's post-secondary education?
(From left): Bill Tatton, the A.S.S. mascot, and William G.

85.0251 (155), University of Calgary Archives

In October of 1958, plans were unveiled for an impressive Calgary campus. Here, some of the province's more influential citizens marvel over a scale model. (From left): Arthur Arnold, Deputy Minister of Public Works; the Honourable E.C. Manning, Premier; the Honourable A.R. Patrick, Minister of Economic Affairs; the Honourable James Hartley, Minister of Public Works; Sigmund Dietze, Project Architect; H.A. Henderson, Chief Architect, D.P.W.

A Bridge to the Future ...

F INANCED BY ENTREPRENEURS WHO HAD MADE their money selling lots in Crescent Heights and sections of land near North Hill, the Centre Street Bridge was erected in 1906. It took a year and a half to build the sturdy concrete bridge. The cost proved to be a bit of a burden. The final tally was an overwhelming $375,000. Consider that in 1909, one of the major grocery supermarkets, Jenkins and Cornfoot at 1229 Ninth Avenue East, only had daily gross sales of approximately $420!

When the Central Street Bridge was completed — with its quartet of concrete lions fashioned after London's famous Trafalgar lions by stonemason James L. Thomson and draftsman Peter Borgesi — it was supposed to spread quite sufficiently above the Bow River. In time, the odd flood threatened to seep over the bridge's lower deck. It was also built outside the city limits. Years later, as the city continued to flourish and grow in size and scope, that would, of course, change.

On December 18, 1916, the first automobile crossed the newly erected Centre Street Bridge. (From left): George W. Craig, City Engineer and John Green, Bridge Engineer.

Glenbow Archives, Calgary, Canada NA-2808-2

Photographer unknown

An Explosive Show!

D URING THE FIRST WEEK OF JULY 1908, Calgary got its first taste of explosive exhibitionism, so to speak. The event was the week-long Calgary Dominion Exhibition. The main attraction at the fairgrounds was Strobel's Airship, an awe-inspiring hydrogen dirigible. This glowing example of the modern age met a premature and fiery end. When the Fourth of July, or "American Day," became particularly windy, Strobel's Airship went flying right into the grandstand and exploded. Although the pilot was badly burned, no one was killed in the accident.

Strobel's airship before ascending into the air, 1908.

Glenbow Archives, Calgary, Canada NA-463-32

Photographer: Byron-May Company Limited, Edmonton, Alberta

A Streetcar Named Disaster

A SURE SIGN OF BIG CITY PROGRESS came in 1909 in the form of Calgary's very first streetcar. Exactly a decade later, one of the streetcars suddenly went wayward ... and crashed straight into Crook's Drug Store on the corner of 17th Avenue and 14th Street South West.

Yet another streetcar accident occurred in 1912 when a McLaughlin-Buick touring car collided with one on 9th Avenue between 1st and 2nd Streets South East.

Glenbow Archives, Calgary, Canada NA-1615-1

(a copy of PB-208-2)

Photographer unknown

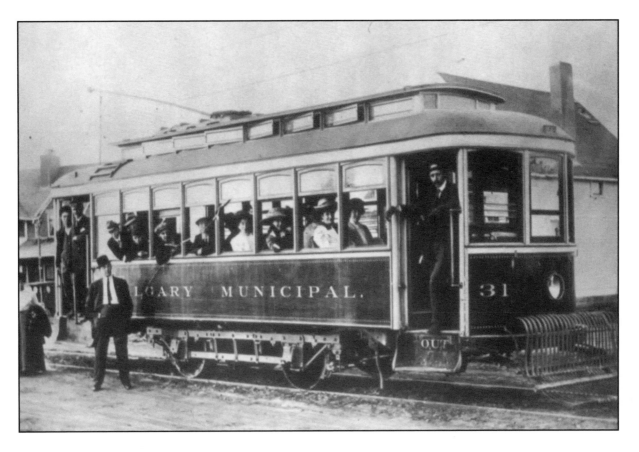

A photograph of Calgary's first streetcar, taken from the vantage point of 26th Avenue and

14th Street South West in 1911.

Glenbow Archives, Calgary, Canada NA-1132-1

Photographer unknown

Calling All Carpenters

A SURE SIGN OF CALGARY'S GROWTH in 1911 could be seen in the burgeoning demand for high quality buildings ... and people to build them! One of the steadiest jobs a person could have was wielding the hammer. The total number of carpenters was greater than any other profession in Calgary.

Nearly a quarter of the city's entire work force found direct employment in the construction sector. There was, after all, a lot of work to be done. Between the years of 1910 to 1912 alone, nearly $40 million was spent on construction projects. The Palliser Hotel contract alone employed five hundred men.

A construction crew working on Calgary's Public Library in 1911.

Included in this snapshot are Peter Mooney (second from left, back row) and Robert McGregor

(second from left, front row). All other names are unknown.

Glenbow Archives, Calgary, Canada NA-1490-2

Photographer unknown

The Calgary of the early 1900s was a city under construction and was definitely moving up in the world. This view of 9th Avenue looking west shows one of its more prominent buildings, the Palliser Hotel, before its glorious completion. This photograph was taken on October 31, 1912.

Glenbow Archives, Calgary, Canada NA-644-13
Photographer: Progress Photo Company, Calgary, Alberta

The City Calgary Could Have Been

THOMAS HAYTON MAWSON WAS AN ACCLAIMED British landscape architect and author who first came to Calgary during a cross-country lecture tour in the spring of 1912. Six months later, Mawson returned, lured by the offer of $6,000 by the town planning commission. His job was to prepare a report addressing comprehensive town planning by April, 1914.

So impressive and stunning in scope was Mawson's report (the full title was *The City of Calgary, Past, Present, and Future* by Thomas H. Mawson and sons, City Planning experts) that one thousand bound volumes of it were produced and sold to the public. The charge for all this extravagance was a mere $2.00 per copy!

Inside this elegantly presented report, the wonders to be witnessed included beautiful boulevards, sprawling open-space parks and river banks, and astonishing designs for buildings. A civic centre planned for a site on the Bow River was said to look like the Kremlin.

While Mawson's report may have been awe inspiring (those who still own a copy will find this collector's item is now worth far more money), the town planning commission was ultimately appalled by the extravagance — especially the estimate that it would cost to $10 million to implement his plan.

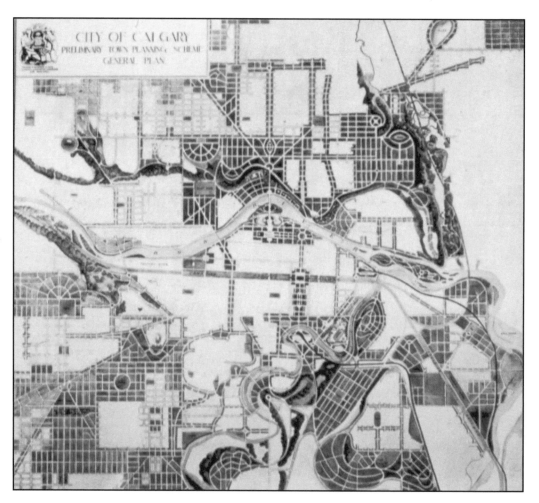

This particular vision for town planning in Calgary comes from the famed Mawson Report of 1912.

Glenbow Archives, Calgary, Canada NA-2018-1

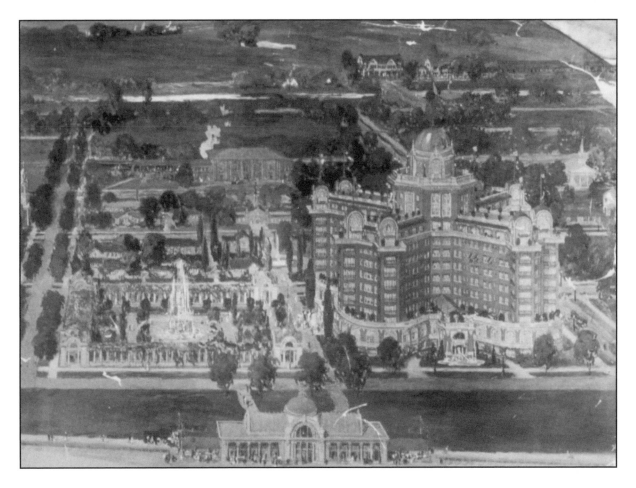

The Civic Centre design from the Mawson Report.

Glenbow Archives, Calgary, Canada NA-1469-55

YEE-HAW!!

Guy Weadick first came to Calgary with the Miller Brothers 101 Ranch Wild West show in 1908 as an American trick roper. So inspired by the experience was Weadick that he couldn't suppress the urge to do it all again — his way. He approached a powerful local figure, CPR livestock agent H. C. McMullen, with the notion of putting on a week-long rodeo in Calgary.

The trick roper's goals were big. The show would include the best cowboys and cowgirls in North America, the most entertaining Western vaudeville acts, and an impressive guest list that included the Duke of Connaught and family.

With big financial backing ($100,000) courtesy of The Big Four (A.E. Cross, Pat Burns, A.J. McLean, and George Lane: a quartet of Calgary's more prominent citizens), Weadick's big gamble was an instant hit. Staged during the annual Calgary Exhibition at the Victoria Park Exhibition Grounds in 1912, the rodeo was referred to, of course, as The Stampede.

Guy Weadick with his wife Flores La Due.

NA-3164-70, Glenbow Museum Archives

Photographer: Oliver, W.J., Calgary, Alberta

In October of 1924, Edward, Prince of Wales, was photographed with Calgary's Big Four.
(From left): Pat Burns, George Lane, the Prince of Wales, A.J. MacLean and A.E. Cross.

Glenbow Archives, Calgary, Canada NA-2043-1

Photographer unknown

It was one wild (and wet) ride. When Miss Carver took a ride on what was billed as "the west's first diving horse," that horse made a spectacular 50-foot leap into a tank of water approximately ten feet deep. Miss Carver stayed on the whole time!

Glenbow Archives, Calgary, Canada NB-16-417
Photographer: Oliver, W.J., Calgary, Alberta

A Love of Leisure

HOW DID THE SOCIAL ELITE OF CALGARY'S pre-war period spend their leisure time? Golfing at the new country club was an elegant affair, if not a fashion show in itself. Parties at ornate city mansions drew select crowds, as did the symphony concerts, music recitals, operas, and plays.

Those with less money to spend, meanwhile, chose a different — and no less thrilling — form of entertainment. They packed theatres to gaze at the latest and most captivating invention from Hollywood: "moving pictures."

Sporting fashions of 1914. (From left): Phoebe Sanders, Archer Toole, William Harris, Mrs. Robert O'Callaghan and Dr. Robert O'Callaghan.

Glenbow Archives, Calgary, Canada NA-2788-66

Photographer unknown

Robert White at Calgary's St. Andrew golf course, circa 1915.

Glenbow Archives, Calgary, Canada PA-3445-4

Photographer unknown

The Princess Theatre, located at 310A — 8th Avenue South East.

Glenbow Archives, Calgary, Canada NA-1469-34

Photographer: Stafford and Kent, Calgary, Alberta

An advertisement for Regal Films and the Capitol Theatre, 1921.

Glenbow Archives, Calgary, Canada NA-2474-3

All of the Splendid Capitol Theatres and Nearly All Other Photoplay Houses in Canada are Presenting the Productions of

Regal Films Limited

Wherever You See Regal Pictures Advertised You Will Find Satisfying Entertainment

THE CALGARY CAPITOL

Western Canada's Greatest Playhouse, will soon offer

BEBE DANIELS in
Oh, Lady, Lady!

An Exceptional Regal Photoplay

Regal Also Releases the Famous Buster Keaton Comedies Which Will Be Shown Exclusively at

THE CALGARY CAPITOL

Regal Films Limited

Calgary, Vancouver, Winnipeg, Toronto, Montreal, St. John

Secret of Success

IN 1913, THERE WAS SPECULATION THAT Freddie Lowes was worth seven million dollars. Born in Brampton, Ontario in 1880, Lowes had come to Calgary in 1902 to become the Alberta representative of the Canada Life Assurance Company. Four years later, he resigned to pursue a career in real estate, opening a small office on Stephen Avenue to the investment tune of $400.

Within five short years, Lowes had successfully opened branches of his business in five Albertan cities, British Columbia, Saskatchewan and Spokane, Washington. Later, he expanded his offices to London, England and New York City.

The secret to Lowes' fame as an entrepreneur was his ability to take wild risks. In order to attract business from Canada and overseas, he would print up promotional literature, transport prospective buyers by train, and tirelessly self-promote himself through the media of any city he was paying a visit to. He wasn't afraid to pay for publicity, either. It was reported that his advertising budget in 1909 was an extravagant $12,000.

Fred C. Lowes, real-estate man, beside Mission Hill
(which was washed down by hydraulic pump to eventually form the
base of the Roxboro subdivision).

Glenbow Archives, Calgary, Canada NA-2957-2
Photographer unknown

In this World War One era view from Freddie Lowes' garden,
soldiers can be seen marching down 30th Avenue South West.

Glenbow Archives, Calgary, Canada NA-479-18

Photographer unknown

The Day It All Went Boom

P REVIOUSLY, THE MAJOR EMPLOYERS OF CALGARY'S able-bodied workers were the CPR and the construction sector. All of that changed on May 14th, 1914. Suddenly, literally over the course of one night, Alberta became oil crazed. Fake companies looking for instant riches printed up important-looking share certificates. The streets were full of sharks in suits and average people with dreams in their eyes.

The man responsible for the frenzy was Archibald Dingman, founder of the Calgary Petroleum Products Company. The company made the first major naphtha-gas discovery in Alberta. The strike occurred in a once quiet stretch of the foothills southwest of Calgary known as Turner Valley. When gas and naphtha spewed out of the ground, Calgary's fate as Canada's oil and gas city was sealed.

The Dingman #1 well in Turner Valley, May 1914.

Glenbow Archives, Calgary, Canada NA-2119-2

Photographer unknown

A photo from *Oil Week* of investors waiting to
purchase oil stocks in 1914.

Glenbow Archives, Calgary, Canada NA-2736-1

World War One

ONLY A FEW MONTHS AFTER THE elation of the Turner Valley oil discovery began, war was declared in Europe on August 4th, 1914. The British Empire was at war and Canadians heard the call to arms. Within the first six weeks of recruitment, over 1,500 Calgarians found themselves en route for a training camp in Valcartier, Quebec before sailing to England.

Two of Calgary's notable infantry divisions were known as "Bell's Bulldogs" (the 31st Battalion of the Canadian Expeditionary Force under Lt. Col. A.H. Bell) and the "Suicide Battalion" (the 50th Battalion under Lt. Col. E.G. Mason).

Isaac Sambrook and his child say goodbye. The year was 1914 and Sambrook was about to leave for France to join in the war effort.

Glenbow Archives, Calgary, Canada NB-50-62
Photographer: Sambrook, I.W., Calgary, Alberta

In 1915, Calgary's Mayor M.C. Costello reviewed the battalion known as "Bell's Bulldogs".
(Officers in front, from left): Major W.H. Hewgill, Lieutenant Colonel A.H. Bell, Major D.R.
Stewart, an unknown soldier, and Captain P.V. Tucker.

Glenbow Archives, Calgary, Canada NA-1189-3

Photographer unknown

In 1914, the Alberta division of the Canadian Red Cross society was created to help soldiers in the war effort. To that end, volunteers and ladies' serving groups were organised to say farewell to troops as they left the train station for the war or to greet them when they returned.

Glenbow Archives, Calgary, Canada NA-3087-2

Photographer unknown

A local campaign collects socks for soldiers overseas as
Ruby Van Sickle and Mary Wilson look on from the window.

Glenbow Archives, Calgary, Canada NA-1567-4

Photographer unknown.

The Battle Against Spirits

"WHISKEY IS ALL RIGHT IN ITS place but its place is in hell." This curious quote from the July 3rd, 1915 edition of *The Calgary Eye Opener* was written by the colourful Bob Edwards. More than a bit of a sipper himself, Edwards was nonetheless highly influential in the vote for total prohibition. While his battle was primarily against the sale of whiskey (he thought beer consumption was fine), many called for a complete ban of liquor.

The plebiscite was set for July 21st. Hoping to swing Edwards over to their side, hotel owners took the writer out and plied him with alcohol. Edwards may have gladly imbibed, but the *Eye Opener* that appeared afterwards was indeed a major eye opener for the bribing entrepreneurs. The controversial writer had suddenly changed his tune. Surprising everyone, Edwards supported full prohibition of alcohol!

Considering the fact that Bob Edwards was known as much for his consumption of alcohol as he was for his strong opinions on politics, it definitely seemed odd when he penned his famous column in support of prohibition. Art Halpen, a fellow member of the Calgary media, claimed that Edwards was under the influence of drink even as he was checking the final proofs of the story.

Along with the rest of the nation, Edwards changed his mind one last time in 1920, requesting that alcohol be taken away from the bootleggers and placed back in the more responsible hands of the government.

This sketch by C.H. Forrester shows a middle class woman's casual response to prohibition: call up your local taxi driver cum criminal and place an order. This satirical cartoon appeared in the summer issue of *The Calgary Eye Opener* in 1922, two years before Alberta's prohibition experiment had ended.

Glenbow Archives, Calgary, Canada NA-2920-6

Bob Edwards, Editor of the *Calgary Eye Opener.*

Glenbow Archives, Calgary, Canada NA-937-12

Photographer unknown

The War is Over

AFTER FOUR YEARS OF BLOODSHED, WORLD War One was finally over in 1918. When the soldiers arrived home, they discovered a foe of an entirely different kind. Those participating in the November 11 victory parade had to wear masks to protect themselves from this deadly enemy.

In 1918, the insidious opponent otherwise known as the Spanish Influenza claimed between twenty and twenty-five million lives around the globe. Those infected by the virus usually died within six months. In Canada, nearly 50,000 deaths were attributed to this disease.

This photograph from the Victory Parade on November 11, 1918

shows the masks worn during the influenza epidemic.

Glenbow Archives, Calgary, Canada NC-20-2

Photographer unknown

An Influential Woman

1918 WAS A WATERSHED YEAR FOR women in politics. Not only did they gain the right to vote in federal elections (Albertan women could vote in provincial elections since 1916), Annie Gale was elected to Calgary's city council.

Annie Gale was no stranger to responsibility or to publicity. During World War One, Gale's work with the Vacant Lots Garden Club ensured that Albertans knew how to grow vegetables as well as their productive neighbours in British Columbia. As an advocate for more responsible pricing of land, food, and housing, Gale encouraged proactive involvement with the Women's Consumer's League and the Women's Ratepayers' Association.

Mrs. Annie Gale, fittingly the captain of this ladies' cricket club,

is seated fourth from left in the second row.

Glenbow Archives, Calgary, Canada NA-2393-2

Photographer: Oliver, W.J., Calgary, Alberta

Building Up Calgary

As CALGARY CONTINUED TO GROW IN size during the early 1900s, construction projects were getting increasingly bigger and more complex. Two important buildings being erected in 1922 included the Institute of Technology, which would house the city's previous Normal School, and the Imperial Oil Company's $2,500,000 oil refinery. During this period, the Imperial Oil Ltd. Royalite No. 4 well was pumping out 500 barrels of "black gold" every day.

On December 2nd, 1922, the Imperial Oil Company plant in Ogden was still under construction.

Glenbow Archives, Calgary, Canada NA-2849-73

Photographer unknown

Spirit of the West

E VEN DURING A DOWNTURN IN THE economy, nothing could hinder the staging of Calgary's most prized annual celebration, the Stampede. The added attractions this time around, introduced by keen-minded promoter Guy Weadick, included chuckwagon racing and flapjack flipping (not so dangerous, but surely as much fun). As well, this was the first year attendants were requested to don their best Old West wear and take their *down-home style* of partying to the streets.

The man with the whiskers is "Billy" Jones, a Canadian Pacific Railway surveyor. He had worked

alongside William Pearce (who was responsible for many of the formative settlement and irrigation

plans in Alberta) on the early land surveys of Western Canada. Here, Billy was one of the "old-

timers" in the Calgary Exhibition and Stampede parade.

Glenbow Archives, Calgary, Canada NB-16-404
Photographer: Oliver, W.J., Calgary, Alberta

The Stampede's famous chuckwagon race.

Glenbow Archives, Calgary, Canada NB(H)-16-265
Photographer: Oliver W.J., Calgary, Alberta

Those Eccentric Artistic Types

CALGARY WASN'T JUST A CITY NOTED for oil barons and chuckwagon riders. It also had its eccentric artsy types to add more colour to life. For example, the acclaimed British artist A.C. Leighton first came to Calgary in 1929. The CPR had hired him to create illustrations and the entire artistic layout for all of its promotional materials.

Another interesting artist — and one who bridged the gap between cowboys and artists — was Charles M. Russell.

The "cowboy artist" Charles M. Russell with the head chief of the Sarcee,

Big Belly, and his wife Maggie.

Glenbow Archives, Calgary, Canada NA-26-2 (same as NC-71-6)

Photographer unknown

Here Comes the Flood

IN 1929, THE LANDSCAPE OF CALGARY'S east side changed dramatically. This time the cause was not the engineering vision or the hard construction work of Calgarians, but the forces of Nature. From the 25th Avenue bridge to the Elbow River, the ground was immersed in a sludgy liquid. St. George's Island and Bowness Park were submerged beneath four feet of water. Calgary's water level rose by 11.8 feet — the highest it had been since the turn of the century.

A Calgary street on 40th Avenue South West

during the flood of 1929.

Glenbow Archives, Calgary, Canada NA-554-32, Glenbow

Photographer unknown

Right to the Senate

During the years she resided in Calgary, the much-lauded author Nellie McClung proved herself to be a controversial, steely character. An advocate for Women's Rights, Prohibition, and even factory safety legislation, McClung was also included in the group known as the "Famous Five." And what was this group famous for? They gained Canadian women the right of appointment to the Senate.

McClung wrote *Purple Springs* and *Painted Fires* while staying in Calgary.

Nellie McClung, photographed circa 1914.

Glenbow Archives, Calgary, Canada NA-1641-1

Photographer unknown

Business as Usual ...?

I N 1929, THE T. EATON COMPANY LAID claim to the corner of Third Street West and Eighth Avenue. Upon this site it erected an impressive store valued at over one million dollars. Another sign of the times was the destruction of the Alexander Corner at 8th Avenue and 1st Street Southwest. The demolition was necessary to make room for a $2.5 million addition to the Hudson's Bay Company's original 1911 structure, located at 7th Avenue and 2nd Street Southwest.

After construction was completed, the Hudson's Bay Company became a particularly impressive and sprawling emporium. Local businessmen wanting to compete against these giant department stores found themselves in the unfortunate predicament of struggling to come up with investment capital and bold new ideas to compete against these heavy hitters.

The T. Eaton Company store, located on 8ᵗʰ Avenue South West between 3ʳᵈ and 4ᵗʰ Streets.

In 1929 and 1930, the store was decorated for the Calgary Exhibition and Stampede.

Glenbow Archives, Calgary, Canada NA-3992-54

Photographer: Oliver, W.J., Calgary, Alberta

The Depression

As 1931 came to a close, CPR's Ogden repair shop — once a major employer in the city — closed its doors, leaving 2,000 Calgarians looking for work. While Turner Valley continued to create employment and farmers fared well during the Depression, the city provided food and shelter for as many as 2,600 single men and 3,200 families.

To add to the traumas of unemployment, December of 1932 brought chilling winds, drifting snow, and ice that together threatened to cause serious damage to key water mains and power lines hidden under the Centre Street Bridge. During this sad, frozen Christmas, advertisements for delicious traditional festive foods no longer appeared. They had been replaced by those of stores desperately trying to sell three cans of soup for a total of twenty-five cents.

The United Married Men's Association takes their message to the streets

(2ⁿᵈ Street East, to be exact).

Glenbow Archives, Calgary, Canada NA-2800-12

Photographer: Tigerstedt, A.F. Calgary, Alberta

The Zoo that Goodwill Built ...

THERE IS NOTHING ODD ABOUT A city bringing its citizens together through the creation and upkeep of a zoo. What was unusual about the Calgary Zoo was how even during the Great Depression, private citizens ensured that the animals were fed and the landmark attraction continued to expand.

It was Dr. O.H. Patrick who envisioned Calgary's world class zoo and formed the Zoological Society in 1928. A labourer named Tom Baines, however, was the one who kept that vision alive during the Depression. Until 1938, Baines performed all the necessary daily duties, from caring for the animals to keeping the grounds clean, almost entirely by himself.

Without the charitable donations from local businesspeople, the zoo Baines cherished so much may never have lasted through the Depression. Baines' friend Lars Willumsen provided the zoo with upgraded facilities. Companies such as Trotter and Morton, Crown Lumber, Beaver and Revelstoke donated free plumbing services and lumber. The budget Baines had for feeding the animals was, to say the least, slim — a mere dollar a day. Thankfully, Pat Burns and Company donated 100 pounds of meat each week while Safeways Ltd. supplied produce.

Tom Baines with his fine-feathered friend (an eagle), 1930.

Glenbow Archives, Calgary, Canada NA-1538-4

Photographer unknown

A lion and lioness at the Calgary Zoo, 1933. They were the first lions in the world to be housed

without heat ... and during a Calgary winter, too!

Glenbow Archives, Calgary, Canada NA-1538-7

Photographer unknown

The Country's Biggest Birthday Cake

THE 75ᵀᴴ BIRTHDAY OF MILLIONAIRE MEAT packer Patrick Burns (July 6, 1931) fell on the opening day of the Calgary Stampede. He was so well loved for his philanthropy that the entire Stampede week was named in his honour. As an additional birthday present, he was given Canada's most enormous birthday cake (a commissioned creation by The Canadian Bakery). It weighed one and a half tonnes, measured eight feet square at the base, and was seven and a half feet high in three tiers.

Burns responded to this flattering gift with an equally big display of kindness. He gave a five pound roast of beef to each of the 2,000 Calgary families who were receiving relief assistance and a 50 cent voucher to each of the 4,000 unemployed single men in the city to be redeemed at any Calgary restaurant or grocery store.

Ingredients of the Patrick Burns Birthday Cake:

4,500 eggs

285 pounds of sugar

304 pounds of butter

380 pounds of flour

12 pounds of spices

115 pounds of raisins

290 pounds of currants

190 pounds each of mixed peel and cherries

80 pounds each of almonds and walnuts

120 pounds of dates

60 pounds of candied pineapple

160 pounds of icing sugar

300 sugar roses

500 sugar lilies

Patrick Burns, photographed here in 1931, was an entrepreneur with a heart.

Glenbow Archives, Calgary, Canada ND-8-14

Photographer: Oliver W.J., Calgary, Alberta

Patrick Burns' wares.

Glenbow Archives, Calgary, Canada NA-1149-4

Photographer unnown

A Return to Horse Power

"Upwardly mobile" would not be a good way to describe the average worker during the Depression. As once flourishing businesses downsized or simply folded up, more and more Calgarians lost their jobs. To help keep families fed and businesses operating, food prices were forced to drop at drastic rates.

Many who were fortunate enough to keep their jobs suffered a drop in their standard of living. When the cost of gas became too much of a burden, motor vehicles became little more than expensive pieces of furniture. That is, unless the owner converted his car into something more economical — such as the Bennett-buggies that were drawn by horses!

A Bennett-buggy in the 1930s.

Glenbow Archives, Calgary, Canada NA-2220-12

Photographer unknown

A Royal Visit

In September 1938, Prime Minister William Lyon Mackenzie King publicly showed his support for British Prime Minister Neville Chamberlain and thanked him for postponing war by allowing Hitler to annex the Sudetenland in Czechoslovakia. Despite this momentary relief, Canadians had begun to accept the possibility that another great war was on the horizon.

During the tense months of anticipation that led up to the war, King George VI and Queen Elizabeth visited Calgary and likely won the support of many Albertans for the future war effort.

On May 26, 1939, King George VI signed the guest book at Calgary's city hall.

Glenbow Archives, Calgary, Canada NA-4325-2 (copied from PD-165)

Photographer: Oliver W.J., Calgary, Alberta

World War Two

MANY CANADIANS STILL SHUDDER AT THE memory of September 1, 1939. On that day, the German attack on Poland began, forcing Britain and France to declare war. In what has become one of the defining moments in Canadian autonomy, Prime Minister King fulfilled his pledge to let the House of Commons decide Canada's course of action. For one week, we remained neutral. Then, on September 10, Canada declared war on Germany.

The first citizen of Calgary to volunteer his patriotic services was a man named Donald McIntyre. During the Second World War, 43 percent of the 178,000 men in Alberta between the ages of eighteen and forty-five enlisted. Of these men, 50,844 joined the Canadian Army, 7,360 joined the Royal Canadian Navy, and 19,499 joined the Royal Canadian Air Force. Troops from across the province reported to Military District 13 headquarters in Calgary.

In 1941, this old sightseeing car was decorated with advertisements for Victory Bonds.

Glenbow Archives, Calgary, Canada NA-1299-3

Photographer unknown

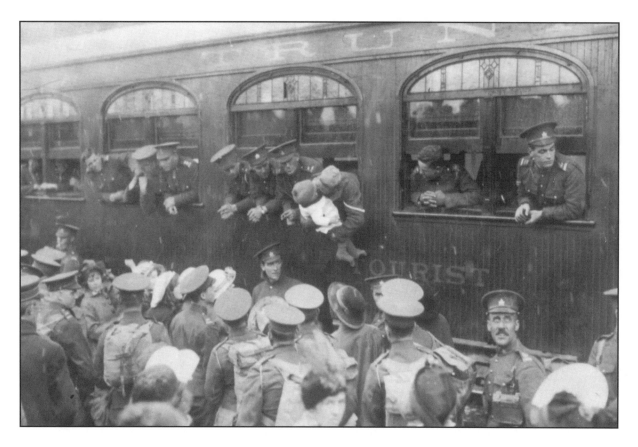

Soldiers saying goodbyes to loved ones.

Glenbow Archives, Calgary, Canada NA-3965-5

Photographer unknown

During this 1942 Victory Bond promotion, a Fairey Moth bomber was put on
display in the lot of a Calgary car dealership.

Glenbow Archives, Calgary, Canada NA-5482-4

Photographer unknown

Fuel for the Front

I T WAS NOT LONG BEFORE YOUNG men and women were on their way to Europe to help in the war effort. The contribution at home could be equally as heroic. As Canada's oil capital, Calgary had an important part to play in the war. As Turner Valley was the only major oil field of its time in Canada and the oil was needed for aeroplane fuel, it only made sense that the province of Alberta was chosen as the centre for the military's air training plan.

By the spring of 1940, over 12,000 troops were training in the Calgary area. In parts of the city, Calgarians could rarely look up at the sky without seeing planes dotting the clouds.

The oil industry, meanwhile, needed workers since so many Albertan men were enlisting in the war effort. During this time, representatives from the oil companies began to pay afternoon visits to nearby high schools. They were looking for any strong students who might be eager to make some money on the weekends. As these were desperate times, no training was required.

What could a wide-eyed, hard-working young farmer's son expect in his new life as a weekend roughneck? Life on the rigs in the 1940s was a time of truly hard work and few comforts — especially during the winter months.

The Dingman Discovery Well, 1913.

Glenbow Archives, Calgary, Canada ND-8-420
Photographer: Oliver W.J., Calgary, Alberta

Workers did not have the down-filled, nylon protective clothing that we have today — indeed, nylon hadn't been invented yet! Woollen underwear and outer clothes were the standard of the day and rarely gave them protection from the bitter cold Albertan winds.

Safety standards were different back then, too. In an age before seat belts, helmets or safety glasses, roughnecks didn't even think of wearing boots with steel toes, let alone flame-resistant outerwear. Young new employees went straight from pitching hay bales to working on the rigs with absolutely no safety training.

Victory came at last in 1945 and World War Two was finally over. Life did not resume as normal for Calgarians, however. The city fell directly into a recession for one long year before the gloom eventually gave way to a boom. On February 13, 1947, just in time for Valentine's Day, Alberta's ongoing love affair with the bubbling, black gold soared to new heights.

After drilling a total of 133 dry holes in Alberta and Saskatchewan, the Imperial Oil Company finally struck something promising on a farm near Leduc just south of Edmonton. It would take about four months and drilling one and half kilometres into the earth for a gusher, however. Then, the famed Leduc Number One blew with a roar of fire and mud, ushering in a new era for Albertan oil.

Not long after Leduc #1 blew, big oil companies from the United States came coveting the drilling rights. Due to its reputation as an oil town, Calgary, and not the much closer Edmonton, found itself playing host to these companies.

While the tycoons played with their big money, a roughneck working on the rigs in 1947 saw wages of just ninety cents an hour.

Leduc Number One blows on Febrary 13, 1947.

COEA EA-10-3164

The Pride of the Pigskin

IN 1948, CALGARY WAS PUT ON the map again, not because of oil but because of pigskin! The Calgary Stampeders had made it to the Grey Cup in Toronto to battle the Ottawa Rough Riders. Not only did the Stampeders prove that the west was best by winning the cup, but they also showed Easterners how to party.

Dressed in full cowboy getups, football fans made the trip down east in a thirteen car train they called the Stampeder Special. The baggage car was packed with six horses, a chuckwagon, and a piano. Proud Calgarians made their mark on the east by having a big chuckwagon breakfast in front of the Royal York Hotel. They even rode a horse through the lobby!

What is particularly impressive about the Calgary Stampeders winning the Grey Cup in 1948 is that the team had only been around for three years. The first time they ever hit the football field was October 22, 1945 to play against the Regina Roughriders at the old Mewata Stadium. Four thousand frenzied fans were there to cheer on their teams. Final score: Calgary, 12, Regina, 0.

The first kick-off of football mania in Calgary dates back to 1909. Back then, a team called the Calgary Tigers was part of the Alberta Rugby Union. Just two years later, the Tigers roared their way to provincial victory when they won the Western Canadian Crown.

Obviously, Calgary's football players were fast learners.

In 1948, Calgary football fans were as full of creativity as they were of pride. Here, four men play the part of pall-bearers for a coffin marked "Ottawa Rough Riders."

Glenbow Archives, Calgary, Canada PA-3471-8
Photographer unknown

On November 30, 1948, 8th Avenue was teeming with fans. During this welcome home parade for the victorious Stampeders, "Sugarfoot" Anderson is being covered with streamers in the lead car. With him are Hood, Strode, and Spaith.

Glenbow Archives, Calgary, Canada NA-3354-9
Photographer: Davis, J., Calgary, Alberta

The Stampede Goes Hollywood

IT WOULD BE PRESUMPTUOUS TO SAY the Calgary Stampede "went Hollywood" during the post-war boom. Actually, the opposite was true — Hollywood was making the trip to Calgary!

During the time when newly struck oil and sudden football heroes had put Calgary more prominently on the map, American celebrities were taking an interest in the city's now world-famous Stampede. Among those who attended the festivities, whether as a guest or perhaps even as a parade marshal, were names as big as Bing Crosby, Bob Hope, Walt Disney, Roy Rogers, and Dale Evans. Even the Cisco Kid made a special appearance.

During the 1959 Calgary Stampede, Bing Crosby brought his family to the grandstand.

Glenbow Archives, Calgary, Canada NA-5093-703

Photographer: Rosettis Studio, Calgary, Alberta

Bovine Illiteracy in Cow Town

R AISING LIVESTOCK ON THE ALBERTAN RANGE was more than a way of life, it was something worth fighting for … especially if you were one of the more forthright farmers like Caroline Fulham. She used to frequent the town's restaurants and hotels looking for leftovers she could use as swill for her prized pigs. Mrs. Fulham also had cows. Unfortunately, one of them wandered onto the CPR tracks one day and was obliterated by an oncoming train.

The CPR soon found that dealing with the cow's owner was like taking on a speeding locomotive. When they claimed that there was a "No Trespassing" sign clearly marked at the tracks, Mrs. Fulham let them have it. Did they really think a *cow* could read? Finally, CPR's management gave her a peace offering: a replacement cow. Fulham took the animal, but would never say a good word about the company.

Photo by: Walker, J. T. St. A.

The Sleepy Hollow School

BETWEEN THE YEARS OF 1901 AND 1911, the population of Calgary grew from 4,000 to 44,000. What people were flocking to was no longer simply a frontier town. The city was rapidly becoming a centre for ranching and agriculture. And, as we know, the Dingman Number One well was soon to blow.

As the city grew, so did the demand for education for the new generation of students. At the turn of the century, schools were often merely classrooms set up in cottages or bungalows. In September of 1903, high school classes were finally separated from elementary classes and moved to two frame buildings on 7th Avenue South East, located just behind what was then City Hall.

The official name of this new school was City Hall School. However, many referred to it by its nickname: "Sleepy Hollow." Inside, there were no science labs, no toilets, and there wasn't even running water.

Education was not often a going concern for either the youths or their parents in the young province. While the lack of facilities and the conditions of schools such as Sleepy Hollow did not exactly encourage attendance, most students were needed on the farms or in the new industries that were springing up.

Despite the lure of quick money or the need to tend to cattle, by 1910, the city had a total of twenty-three schools. Five years later, post secondary education was given support when the Alberta Provincial Institute of Technology and Arts opened its doors.

And the band played on ... A dance band from Central High School in Calgary plays in the orchestra pit of the Palace Theatre. (From left to right): Norman Dunn, George F.G. Stanley, Reginald Hart, N. Clarke Wallace.

Glenbow Archives, Calgary, Canada NA-2968-28
Photographer unknown

At the official opening of the University of Alberta, Calgary gymnasium in 1962, Andy Vangoor demonstrates the value of Phys. Ed. for Mrs. Pat Cain (left), Y.W.C.A. Physical Director, and Miss Elaine Liebert (right), student.

82.010, University of Calgary

A Bright Idea!

THE PIONEERS WHO FIRST LIVED IN Calgary back in 1886 couldn't possibly have known what a shock they would get the following year. In 1887, a mysterious element — simultaneously dangerous, fascinating, and extremely useful — arrived in town: electricity.

It was ex-mountie James Walker who, in 1885, became a pioneer of the new Electrical age. He connected his lumber company office at Stephen Avenue and his sawmill operation east of the Elbow River with telephones.

Just two years later, on September 2, the Calgary Electric Lighting Company Limited was incorporated and soon began lighting up the community with a low voltage direct current.

In this tug-of-war between Sarcee and Stoney women, the great overseer of deeds, Colonel James Walker, played the role of umpire.

Glenbow Archives, Calgary, Canada NB-16-577
Photographer: Oliver, W.J., Calgary, Alberta

Writing Off into the Sunset

ODAY, CALGARY IS A CITY BURSTING with prosperity and personality. It remains one of the country's most powerful energy centres. Calgary and its surrounding areas boast the largest oil and gas production in Canada. Over time, it has become renowned as the business capital of Western Canada. What was once a small frontier town in a land considered best left to the trapper is now home to the second highest amount of head offices in the entire country.

Truly, the "Cow Town" of old has diversified and blossomed into an impressive urban centre with bustling downtown streets. Consistently, Calgary has met the challenges of employment, industry, and commerce. And the number of "new pioneers" settling here in the twenty-first century is as staggering as it is impressive. It is expected that Calgary's population will grow to over a million people by the year 2007.

While it is true the city's earliest settlers could never have imagined the Calgary of today, something else is true: some things never change.

Every summer, you can rest assured that Calgarians and international visitors alike will don their best cowboy clothes and watch good, old-time chuckwagon races. Or they will flock to the midway for some candy floss, a

corn dog, maybe a candied apple and few amusement park rides. Indeed, the Calgary Stampede is alive, well, and kicking up an internationally acclaimed storm.

Relics of a more ancient past still remain, too. The Calgary Zoo, created with such vision and passion during the Depression, is one of the largest zoos in all of North America. Dinny the Dinosaur, its famous Brontosaurus statue brought to life back in 1934, still stalks the earth.

With its eyes focused on the future, Calgary enters the twenty-first century much as it did the last: full of promise and potential. Calgary will continue to grow. Calgary will continue to prosper. Calgary will continue to play an increasingly important role in North America. The pioneering spirit that made a city rise up out of the rich Albertan soil has only begun to test its potential. After all, Calgary is still a very young city.

If we can imagine John Glenn travelling to the future, seeing our world while we stare into these photographs from a time gone by, then perhaps we can imagine our great, great grandchildren looking at our own pictures. In our photographs they would surely see glimpses of the pioneering spirit of Calgary.

Bibliography

Calgary 100: 100 Year History of Calgary. Calgary: Provost Promotions & Publications Ltd., 1974.

Calgary Stampeders. Marketing and Communications. *Calgary Stampeders 1998 Grey Cup Champions 1999 Media Guide*. Ron Rooke, Vice President, Editor and Publisher, 1999.

Dempsey, Hugh A. *Calgary, Spirit of the West*. Saskatoon: Fifth House Publishers, 1994.

Foran, Max and Heather MacEwan Foran, *Calgary: Canada's Frontier Metropolis, An Illustrated History*. Windsor: Windsor Publications, Inc., 1982.

Foran, Max. *The History of Canadian Cities: Calgary An Illustrated History*. (Photos assembled by Edward Cavell), James Lorimer & Company, Publishers, Ottawa: and National Museum of Man, National Museums of Canada, Halifax: 1978.

McNeill, Leishman. *The Calgary's Herald's Tales of the Old Town*. Calgary: The Calgary Herald, Lithographed in Canada by Canniff Printing (1964) Ltd., 1966.

Peach, Jack. *Thanks for the Memories, More Stories from Calgary's Past*. Saskatoon: Fifth House Publishers, 1994.

Rasporich, Anthony W. and Henry C. Klassen. *Frontier Calgary: Town, City and Region 1875-1914*. Calgary: McClelland and Stewart West, 1975.

Stacey, C.P. *Arms, Men & Governments: The War Policies of Canada, 1939-1945*. Ottawa: Queens Printer, 1970.

Stenson, Fred. *The Story of Calgary*. Saskatoon: Fifth House Publishers, 1994.

About the Authors

M ARK KOZUB IS AN EXPERIENCED FREELANCE magazine writer for a wide variety of publications, ranging in focus from business to arts and entertainment.

Janice Kozub is a professional freelance writer and speech writer for the Government of Alberta.